Healing Workshop:

A Manual Blessed By Angels

Angelic Request Therapy

By
Angela Raasch

The author of this book does not dispense medical advice or prescribe the use of any technique as a form of treatment for physical or medical problems without the advice of a doctor either directly or indirectly. The intent of the author is only to offer information of a general nature to help you in your quest for emotional and spiritual wellbeing. In the event you use any of the information in this book for yourself, which is your right, the author and the publisher assume no responsibility for your actions.

First published in Great Britain in 2013 by Angelic Workshop

www.angelicrequesttherapy.com
angelicworkshop@btinternet.com

ISBN: 978-1484196427

First Edition

ACKNOWLEDGEMENTS

To my husband Steve, sons, daughters and the angelic force that guide me, a huge thank you for your patience and love, without you all my life would be colourless & totally unfulfilled.

Acknowledgement must also be given to Helen Berlouis for painstakingly correcting my English!

Lastly to the Virtues, who have channelled this information to benefit all; bless you.

ABOUT THE AUTHOR

Angela Raasch, daughter, wife, mother and friend has channelled this work over a summer. This is her first manual, giving mankind information to alleviate personal suffering, allowing all access to Universal healing. Coming to work within the healing field over the last few years has allowed Angela understanding of fellow emotional pain. Her own life path has given knowledge that all first-hand trials cannot be avoided yet can be used as a bench mark for growth.

The power of requesting Angelic aid in life helps to allow, all who do so, understanding that the care of mankind, the planet and all of her creatures are the upper most concern of the angelic force. Angela has been tasked with bringing this information to reach as many as possible, bringing hope to all, alleviating the journey through life so every person alive may experience joy and other positive qualities.

This method of Angelic healing is extremely simple, requiring all who try to just 'ask' aloud, a practice that has been forgotten over the last few generations, regardless of religious belief or personal circumstances the Angelic kingdom wish to assist all.

CONTENTS

FOREWORD 1

CHAPTER 1 5
RELEASING PAST PAINFUL MEMORIES..5
SACRED CIRCLE OF ANGELIC BEINGS 6

CHAPTER 2 9
RELATIONSHIPS...9
REQUEST FOR TRANSMUTING NEGATIVE ENERGY............................14
REQUEST FOR DISSOLVING INCANTATIONS 15
REQUEST FOR DISSOLVING RECEIVED CURSES 16
REQUEST FOR TRANSMUTING NEGATIVE ENERGY I HAVE SENT........17
REQUEST FOR DISSOLVING A PERSONAL CORD..................................18
REQUEST FOR TRANSMUTING CREATED KARMA 19

CHAPTER 3 21
RELEASING VOWS/OATHS/PACTS/CURSES/INCANTATIONS...............21
REQUEST FOR RELEASING VOWS 23
REQUEST FOR RELEASING OATHS 24
REQUEST FOR RELEASING PACTS 25
REQUEST FOR RELEASING CURSES 26
REQUEST FOR RELEASING INCANTATIONS(SPELLS) 27

CHAPTER 4 29
KARMA...29
REQUEST FOR DISSOLVING KARMIC DEBT INCURRED WITHIN THIS
LIFETIME 31
REQUEST FOR DISSOLVING KARMIC DEBT INCURRED FROM PAST
LIFETIMES 32
FAMILY KARMA 33
REQUEST FOR DISSOLVING INHERITED KARMIC DEBT (MATERNAL)... 35
REQUEST FOR DISSOLVING INHERITED KARMIC DEBT (PATERNAL) 36

CHAPTER 5 37
MIASMS 37
REQUEST FOR TRANSMUTING MIASMS 39
MIASM DEBRIS 40
REQUEST FOR TRANSMUTING MIASM DEBRIS..................................42
REQUEST FOR TRANSMUTING MIASM DEBRIS WITHIN BUILDINGS ..43

REQUEST FOR TRANSMUTING MIASM DEBRIS FOR ANOTHER 44
MIASMS AQUIRED THROUGH KARMA 45
REQUEST FOR RELEASE FROM KARMIC DEBT 46
REQUEST FOR RELEASE FROM INHERITED MIASMS 47
UNWANTED ENERGY 48
REQUEST FOR DISSOLVING RECEIVED NEGATIVE ENERGY 49
REQUEST FOR DISSOLVING PERSONALLY SENT NEGATIVE ENERGY ...50

CHAPTER 6 51
AKASHIC RECORD 51
REQUEST FOR CONNECTION BETWEEN YOUR AKASHIC RECORD AND
YOUR RECORDING ANGEL 54

CHAPTER 7 55
DISTANT HEALING 55
REQUEST FOR DISTANT HEALING 57
REQUEST FOR HEALING ACCIDENTAL INJURY 58

CHAPTER 8 59
SICK EARTH ENERGIES 59
    SICK BUILDING SYNDROME 59
REQUEST FOR RESTORING POSITIVE ENERGY TO HOUSE OR BUILDING
.... 61
    ELECTRICAL EFFECT ON BUILDINGS 62
REQUEST TO CHANGE TECHNOPATHIC STRESS INSIDE
HOMES/BUILDINGS 63
    OUTSIDE EARTH ENERGIES 64
REQUEST FOR POSITIVELY CHANGING OUTSIDE EARTH ENERGIES 66
REQUEST FOR TRANSMUTING TECHNOPATHIC STRESS OUTSIDE 67

CHAPTER 9 69
PROTECTION 69
PROTECTION REQUEST FOR PERSONAL RELATIVES 73
PROTECTION REQUEST FOR PERSONAL USE 74
PROTECTIVE REQUEST FOR NEIGHBOURHOOD 75
PROTECTIVE REQUEST FOR HOME/WORKPLACE 76
PROTECTIVE REQUEST FOR SCHOOLS/HOSPITALS/COMMUNITY 77
HALLS 77

CHAPTER 10 79
PLANETARY HEALING 79
HEALING REQUEST TO RELIEVE OUR PLANET 82
HEALING REQUEST TO RELIEVE THE SEAS, OCEANS, ALL WATERS......83
AND LAND..83
HEALING REQUEST TO RELIEVE STRESS FROM PLANET EARTH...........84

FOREWORD

The human race has been provided with Divine assistance, so that each man, woman and child may be aided throughout their life, allowing all who ask benevolence, protection, access to healing, and the ability to sustain healthy relationships which benefit one and all; taking all those who use their personal angelic support to new levels, allowing the journey through life to nourish every step of the way. Finding the method of communication to these heavenly bodies creates a fruitful link, which will endeavour to enhance those who choose to take full advantage of their invisible celestial supporters. Reading through this workshop manual will give you information to establish a life filled with many friends, to keep one's home a safe, vibrant base, to assist the planet, to release your karmic debts and send healing unobtrusively, to access your own Akashic record, and to remove all unwanted nullifying energy.

There is only one obstacle preventing Angelic aid, and that is the personal trials you may have chosen to enable growth before you were born. In these instances, Angelic hands are tied, but may at least give assistance in smoothing the incident once experienced, enabling swift recovery. This also applies if you are concerned over another's trials; requesting help for them allows the person relief. Angelic balm can be given for complete healing of situations causing grief or confrontation, relieving all concerned. However, if it must be experienced then nothing will stop this process; once the incident has occurred then all that can be given to alleviate those involved, will be.

How do you decide on a relevant request? Reading chapter headings will be the first indication as to the appropriate area relevant to your own predicament. Noticing titles that leap off the page at you indicates a need for investigation. Give yourself time to take on board coincidences that repeat. Often, your higher mind is at work trying to communicate concerns. Gut-feeling goes a long way to realising personal truths. In our impatient modern world, we have produced an expectant society, preoccupied with instant results, which as a consequence no longer listens to its inner emotions. However, these emotions still battle for our attention when something is amiss. Some people are naturally adept at using age-old methods of connecting to their own inner voice through dowsing. This would be a most appropriate skill for anyone to develop, but requires patience to master.

Once a selection has been made, it is important to follow these simple guidelines to ensure success. Always find a quiet place where you will not be disturbed. Repeat the chosen request aloud, ensuring you include the relevant archangel or, where indicated, the name for your own personal 'God' figurehead, then sit or stand quietly whilst the request is acted upon. Some may feel the energy go through their system; make sure your limbs are straight with feet flat on the floor. Once complete, take time out for yourself, and drink plenty of water. Remember, this is a process of change, taking a few days to settle into your being. Make allowance for the process to filter through all aspects of your life, and then enjoy expanding every area, fulfilling your journey.

CHAPTER 1

RELEASING PAST PAINFUL MEMORIES

Letting go of the past, (both painful memories and deep-seated hurts), is an incredible releasing mechanism enabling future growth, realising inner peace, and seeding future happiness. If you find yourself looking back at life with difficulty for whatever reason, realise that you are not living fully or taking charge of your own destiny, because your past experiences have, in effect, created stalemate.

This also applies to adult exposure to negative incidence; for example, relationships that resulted in pain of whatever kind, or accidental incidence that has resulted in bad memories. Releasing all negative experience enables you to take charge of your life again.

Life is precious and meant to be filled with fulfilment not wasted in fear.

As a sacred symbol, the circle depicts one's journey of life. Utilising the power of this symbol can have a benevolent effect in aiding those seeking personal change, you can re-establish balance, bring completeness and provide a forward momentum into whatever future you wish to co-create. A combination of Archangels and twelve intuitively chosen crystals aids this powerful healing.

SACRED CIRCLE OF ANGELIC BEINGS

1. Make a circle using 12 intuitively chosen crystals
2. Address this circle of stones either silently or aloud, requesting each crystal to link with the others to create a circle of energy. Allow two minutes for this grid to establish
3. Sit yourself in the centre of the circle facing the direction of sunrise
4. It is now time to call in the first Archangel, Raphael. Address each of the four Archangels so:

"I request that Archangel Raphael stand in front of me"
Repeat request 3 times

Remain still once you have called in each of the Archangels, sensing the individual energy each one brings:

"I request that Archangel Gabriel stand behind me"
Repeat request 3 times

"I request Archangel Michael stand on my right-hand side"
Repeat request 3 times

"I request Archangel Uriel stand on my left-

hand side"

Repeat request 3 times

5. Imagine now that a golden six-pointed star is slowly descending over you; bringing you deep calm, filling every cell of your being with Divine Light, transmuting bad memories stored within your heart centre, and every individual system that makes your physical body. This releasing process may take up to 15 minutes to complete. Be aware of emotions that may arise. This is part of the process. Understand that these thoughts can no longer be accepted; transforming can take place if you do **not** try to hold on to any stray thought. Instead, allow all to flow away from you

6. Silently or aloud, ask all four Archangels simultaneously:

"Divine Grace flow through my being, replenish all that has been removed"

Allow time for your restored body to settle down once more.

7. Ask for the Archangels to place you in a protective bubble. Thank each Archangel as they now leave

8. Remove the stone circle, rest, and drink plenty of fresh mineral water

CHAPTER 2

RELATIONSHIPS

Establishing harmonious relationships with all who share our lives creates a supportive network for everyone involved. These relationships begin with family ties and often are the hardest to maintain. They form in the cradle from the very first breath, influencing one's entire life. These basic relationships enable everyone, allowing success for all future connections. Those who do not have this basic framework, for whatever reason, must understand that knowledge of family does not always have to mean mother/father interconnection; any guiding adult can play a developmental role.

Adult relationships then become a teaching ground for children, repeating throughout lifetimes. When two people befriend, they acknowledge that they want to form lasting companionship based on mutual agreement, forming a cord between the two. The cord is an invisible link, which, when damaged, can end the association. If cleansed, it can also remove detrimental energy, preventing further deterioration. The cord is a vital connection, giving both people necessary shared interests, building on a lifetime of association, and thus allowing each person to create a foundation.

When one person outgrows the friendship and tries to break free, the cord remains in place holding everything in suspension. When they meet again, the friendship is rekindled as though they had never been apart.

Couples who have violence within their relationship, for example, find it hard to break the link because their cord is strong. Many go back into harmful situations not realising that nothing will change until the energy of the cord is dissolved, which instantly frees both people to move on.

Personal relationships between couples form a connection the minute they rise above all others, and is given blessed energy when married, (this includes matrimony occurring within all faiths, civil marriages and religions). When the marriage fails, the cord remains intact. An ex-marital partner finds herself/himself unknowingly connecting to similar partners, and, without realising, subsequently going over the same ground with the new spouse, keeping both parties constantly going round in circles. Completely dissolving these cords becomes essential if all wish to move on.

It is common to find that if a person's subconscious mind decides to separate from their partner, they behave in the role of victim, thereby creating the very outcome perceived.
For example if a wife thinks that her husband

will eventually cheat on her, that energy is given form; he subconsciously connects to it and then goes looking for another.

When friendship is formed it is important to be positive right from the outset, setting strong bonds. Any notion of limiting the relationship will do just that - limit it, thereby creating shaky foundations, which will in time cause upset. Being positive in all aspects of life makes one happy, strong and attractive to others, who will then wish to connect to you, enabling your enthusiasm to spread to all you meet. You will find that you then draw to you happy and enthusiastic people, giving you a large selection of like-minded souls whom you can rely on.

Friendships that have become strained in some way through either one party or the other will flounder if left. Transmuting the cord with benevolent energy is a natural solution, as it dissolves all negativity that has developed within the relationship, and also endows the friendship with fresh vigour.

Friendships established with one party harbouring ideas of manipulation or control of the other needs balance and equilibrium added before they implode. Once more, transmuting the cord corrects what is necessary to move forward.

In this day and age, many still choose to use witchery when all else has failed, in order to secure a controlling element using incantations. These individuals are best left alone to their own fate. Calling in an Archangel to dissolve the cord completely is vital in removing all connecting energy. Not all who follow natural craft take this path of using their gift in such a negative way. Another cynical, sinister method that is deliberately aimed to cause hurt, and which should be considered here, is that of 'cursing' another. Cursing creates very nullifying energy that pervades the very being of another with its wishes; even if it were meant light-heartedly, the energy is still created with that purpose in mind. Be aware of your own behaviour in this instance, as you will earn karma. If you have in the past cursed another, and wish to evoke your deed by dissolving both the curse and the karma, you can request angelic help to do so.

All relationships require work at times, especially those formed at birth. These are usually the most trying in life. Our closest family often provides lessons that are needed within this lifetime. If you can take on board just that; that these are required personal lessons, then familial relationships may become reasoned, and hopefully understood. You do not need to live your life in relationships that compromise your freedom. However, if you choose to help those loved ones who need assistance, then that is personal growth, which enables both learning *and* assistance.

Keeping a positive flow within all of your relationships allows a healthier, happier and more supportive existence for everyone. Simply asking for Angelic support in endeavouring to maintain this endorses a lifetime full of meaningful relationships.

REQUEST FOR TRANSMUTING NEGATIVE ENERGY

"Archangel Zadkiel,

I thank you for transmuting all negative energy benevolently between myself and ………. restoring Grace, blessing myself and ………. with Violet Fire, divine beneficial relationship between us both.

Thank You"

Repeat this request aloud 3 times

REQUEST FOR DISSOLVING INCANTATIONS

"Archangel Metatron,

I ask that you dissolve benevolently all incantations I have received, and restore all of my energy, divine beneficial friendships from now on. I ask that you also dissolve all connection to the individual concerned.

Thank You."

Repeat this request aloud 3 times

REQUEST FOR DISSOLVING RECEIVED CURSES

"Archangel Metatron,

I ask that you dissolve all curses that I have received from men, women, children, and the physical thrist of my enemies benevolently. Please will you restore Grace to my being. Bring divine relationships from now on.

Thank You."

Repeat this request aloud 3 times

REQUEST FOR TRANSMUTING
NEGATIVE ENERGY I HAVE SENT

"Archangel Metatron,

I ask that all negative energy that I have sent .... be transmuted benevolently. Restore .... giving her/him divine Grace.
Please benevolently transmute our cord with positive divine energy, allowing friendship once more.

Thank You."

Repeat this request aloud 3 times

REQUEST FOR DISSOLVING A PERSONAL CORD

"Archangel Michael,

I ask that you dissolve my cord with .... benevolently with Grace. Please bring divine healing to both myself and .... allowing us both to move on. Divine relationships from now on.

Thank You."

Repeat this request aloud 3 times

REQUEST FOR TRANSMUTING
CREATED KARMA

"Archangel Metatron,

I ask that you transmute the karma I have earned for the deeds that I carried out against ……… with Grace. Please restore ……… and my own being. Divine relationships from now on.

Thank You."

Repeat this request aloud 3 times

CHAPTER 3

RELEASING VOWS/OATHS/PACTS/
CURSES/INCANTATIONS

Making any marital promise creates a life-long agreement to remain faithful to those vows. This mutual, willing exchange binds two people together throughout their lifetime. When the partnership fails to the extent of separation and divorce, both are still held together by the cord initiated at the start of the relationship. This cord will remain between the couple until one passes, regardless of any other new romance. The vow created energy, and this energy makes new associations difficult, to the extent that further partnerships often follow repetitive patterns until the original promise is released, when all are free to move on. Words are powerful; they create energy, which ensures successful momentum. If a religious element were part of the occasion, then the couple would also receive a blessing of Grace to secure the matrimonial energy. Asking for assistance when all else has failed, releases marital ties. Be aware of your commitments to any future relationship so that you do not also end your life with karmic debt for irresponsible behaviour.

Ceremony of any kind creates energy from a simple act of children binding together as 'blood brothers/sisters' to swearing an oath of allegiance. The words spoken remain in one's entire being until one passes. Sometimes they can remain with you throughout lifetimes, hindering any form of progress. Oaths, pacts, curses and incantations or spells that have been made, allow negative influence into either your own or another's life. If this energy is allowed to remain, the person concerned is blighted by whichever nullifying category that is in play.

Previous lifetimes have seen people experience different time periods where it may have been commonplace to make oaths, pacts and incantations: oaths of revenge between families or clans, swearing allegiance to fight for a cause, taking the oath of chastity for religious purposes, (or other reasons such as poverty), or simply cursing another or an entire village, causing negating energy to permeate the very foundations of families or communities. You may not consider this important information if you have no previous knowledge of past-life influence, but nevertheless it could be the very element preventing your passage in one area of your life. Look very carefully at your own life. Identify areas that are simply not working for you and consider the possibility of previous incarnations blocking any particular area. Angelic aid is considerable when working in these fields.

REQUEST FOR RELEASING VOWS

"Archangel Metatron,

Please benevolently release all previously made divine Vows from all lifetimes with Grace. I ask that you bless this soul with benevolent energy allowing exemption of Vow.

Thank You."

Repeat this request aloud 3 times

REQUEST FOR RELEASING OATHS

"Archangel Metatron,

Please benevolently release all Oaths that I have made from all lifetimes with Grace; freeing me of all commitment. I ask that I may receive benevolent blessing giving divine energy for release of all Oaths.

Thank You."

Repeat this request aloud 3 times

REQUEST FOR RELEASING PACTS

"Archangel Metatron,

Please benevolently release all previous Pacts made from all lifetimes with Grace.
I ask that I may receive benevolent blessing giving divine energy for release of all Pacts.

Thank You."

Repeat this request aloud 3 times

REQUEST FOR RELEASING CURSES

"Archangel Metatron,

Please benevolently release all previous Curses made from all lifetimes with Grace. I ask that I may receive benevolent blessing giving divine energy for release of all Curses.

Thank You."

Repeat this request aloud 3 times

REQUEST FOR RELEASING
INCANTATIONS (Spells)

"Archangel Metatron,

Please benevolently release all previous Incantations from all lifetimes with Grace; giving my soul blessing from negative energy and divine energy for release from all Incantations.

Thank You."

Repeat this request aloud 3 times

CHAPTER 4

KARMA

Understanding life and the journey embarked upon gives everyone a clear grasp of the meaning of 'Karma'. If you can take on board the idea that you have chosen to be born at this moment in time, selecting your parents, your pathway, your own characteristics and abilities, before you were ever planned or conceived, then you must also recognize that all of this meticulous planning had a purpose. Previous incarnations experienced have shaped you; gaining you both good and detrimental aspects that you need to work on during this lifetime, in order to give you a chance to improve. The journey is as simple as that. Once recognition is understood, it becomes one manageable riddle, with information enabling progression.

In this lifetime, choice is given so that everyone who wishes can ask for divine cleansing; leaving past karmic debt, and allowing a fresh start. This has been granted so that we may raise our vibration, which in turn assists the planet to evolve. Clearing one's karmic slate permits all to benefit those that have been due Karma from past deeds done to them; they no longer have to engage with their debtor during this lifetime, freeing them for better experiences. Likewise, those that have karmic debt to pay are freed as well. Any Karma accrued from the point of cleansing, will, however, be swiftly settled within this life.

Allowing karmic debt to be disposed of gives the person involved the ability for growth. Indeed they may raise their own awareness to the point of lifting their vibration. This in turn those closest to them, enabling their own awareness to grow, like a pebble rippling on a pond. The effect expands outwards, bringing good vibrations to one and all. When this occurs, changes in the way people think begin to take shape, creating positive experiences. Day-to-day occurrences and life in general becomes more pleasurable. The personal life changes made by one will extend to the lives of those around them, i.e. family, friends and work colleagues. In conclusion one person changes the action lifts the burdens of others. Adjusting to new feelings is part of this process, which, once begun, has a wonderful tendency for change: giving new direction, purpose, reason for continuance, finding a way forward without carrying heavy millstones, leaving behind karmic debts, freeing the path of the future, and in doing so, allowing a person a lifetime of growth.

REQUEST FOR DISSOLVING KARMIC DEBT INCURRED WITHIN THIS LIFETIME

"Archangel Metatron,

I ask that you benevolently release all Karmic Debt incurred within my lifetime, allowing both myself and those that have gained penalties and rightful reason to repay Grace, transmuting all that is owed, blessing each person.

Thank You."

Repeat this request aloud 3 times

REQUEST FOR DISSOLVING KARMIC DEBT INCURRED FROM PAST LIFETIMES

"Archangel Metatron,

I ask that you benevolently release all Karmic Debt incurred from all other lifetimes allowing both myself and those that have gained penalties and rightful reason to repay Grace, transmuting all that is owed, blessing each person.

Thank You."

Repeat this request aloud 3 times

FAMILY KARMA

Your family connection provides your very first influence, thereby shaping your life. Childhood guidance affects your thoughts and actions during your formative years, helping to give you a framework to build on. Expectations, values, traditions and familial peculiarities are passed down through generations naturally, verbally and through observation. Orphaned children have dual influence; that of the new family, and, in addition, instinctively inherited traits, which may play a part within a person's life.

Family Karma may be inherited as well. Karmic influence affects all members of a family unit, even if subtly it still remains. The cause may be long forgotten, but the initial intent remains in place, affecting new generations. Asking for divine assistance removes all negative aspects from a complete family line. In removing all trace forevermore, you provide the chance to give future generations new experiences, also allowing past generations relief from karma created as a direct result. Requesting assistance for Family Karma to be transmuted allows healing for the whole line, thereby benefiting many. Once this has occurred, future generations may be free to experience life unhampered, so giving them a chance to reach their full potential. You may have issues with family members, which prevent you from wanting the best for these individuals. Understand that your problems will be put to one side whilst the whole picture is addressed. You cannot omit any person at will, no matter what they have done. Likewise, you can request your family of in-laws be assisted in the same way, allowing your own offspring a chance to fully benefit.

Family Karma can be as simple as all members experiencing life as pig-headed, or set in their ways. Alternatively, at the other end of the scale, members may never achieve wealth, abundance in any form, or payment in full; making life unnaturally hard for generations, and preventing the growth of an entire family. These scenarios differ, from the personal choice of one individual to experience poverty in all its forms, or any other negative trait throughout one's current lifetime, to an entire family, dating back through generations, always experiencing the same situation.

This simple act enables families to experience life unhindered by the past.

REQUEST FOR DISSOLVING INHERITED KARMIC DEBT
(Maternal)

"Archangel Metatron,

I ask that you benevolently release all Karmic Debt incurred by my mother's family and those that have gained penalties and rightful reason to repay Grace, allowing those persons peace, freeing all; allowing this family to be blessed with Grace.

Thank You."

Repeat this request aloud 3 times

REQUEST FOR DISSOLVING INHERITED KARMIC DEBT
(Paternal)

"Archangel Metatron,

I ask that you benevolently release all Karmic Debt incurred by my father's family and those that have gained penalties and rightful reason to repay Grace, allowing those persons peace, freeing all; allowing this family to be blessed with Grace.

Thank You."

Repeat this request aloud 3 times

CHAPTER 5

MIASMS

Miasms, or detrimental influence, can play a leading role in casting a negative shadow over one's life. Recognising unusual, nullifying, cynical, gloomy, disregarding behaviour that has suddenly directed your life in your thoughts and actions helps to identify a change in your being. Understanding that you are no longer your usual self, but cannot identify when these changes began to creep into your everyday thought patterns and making daily life no longer pleasant, allows you to understand you may be unwillingly hosting negative force. There is an exception to this being 'chemical depression' where the imbalance of serotonin in the body has caused a negative reaction.

We are bodies of light. Unfortunately, only a few have the ability to 'see' all aspects of the human field, as the Universe is able to. Given this ability, individuals would experience a complete revelation and newfound understanding of how we are truly aspected. Lamentably, other life forces are able to distinguish this light, and are consequently drawn to influence whoever they can. Over many months, this influence can play a very destructive part, affecting not only the original person, but also anyone who shares their life, again, like a pebble in a pond rippling outwards. Many have strong enough personalities to overcome such undesirable effect. A certain few, however, at low points in their lives, (i.e., those who use drugs or drink, leaving their naturally vibrant physical selves vulnerable,) leave themselves open to such sway. It is very common in this day and age to be influenced in such a way. Many carry on daily without realising how they have changed. Until someone points out the changes, they feel perfectly normal, just gloomier than usual. Taking steps to ensure protection is carried out on a regular basis, gives an individual control, allowing life to be experienced to the full.

REQUEST FOR TRANSMUTING MIASMS

"Creator,

I ask that you benevolently bless my being with white Light to transmute all unwanted presences, removing presences to an appropriate place, leaving them without chance to move to another. Restore Grace in all of my being, giving vitality again.

Thank You."

Repeat this request aloud 3 times

MIASM DEBRIS

Once contaminated, the human field requires extra consideration that of transmuting all necessary areas touched by any miasm. This process is required to ensure that all trace be removed, thereby allowing complete purified change, giving the individual a chance to return to normality.

One must understand one aspect of these phenomena and that is the personal creating of negative energy. It must be understood that all will benefit from this knowledge. Any individual creates their own reality daily: through thoughts, dreams, words and actions. If one thinks negatively about oneself, then this creates the energy to bring about that thought form, shaping that thought into reality. Hence, if you repeatedly think that you are going to be sacked from your job, eventually you will, in effect, make it happen just by thinking it. If you continually think negative thoughts about yourself in any way, these become your reality. Consequently, if you think dark thoughts about others or yourself, this energy creates a dark mass around you, tainting not only yourself, but also your home, your surrounding environment, and all those who share this space with you. A vicious circle is formed and once it takes hold, it becomes hard to break free; affecting one and all, preventing yourself and all those connected to you from discovering their true path to happiness. You may have experienced this when visiting a place that has been indoctrinated with this form of negative vibration; one which has saturated the very walls you are surrounded by, leaving you feeling very uncomfortable indeed. You may also feel drawn to avoid certain people, as once again you feel very uncomfortable within their presence. Be aware at all times of your feelings, gut instincts, whatever you wish to call it, as this helps you to identify negative aspects.

Every form of negative energy can be transmuted. Understanding your own part in its creation is vitally important. Positive thinking about yourself, the people you share your life with and your environment is crucial for you to maintain fulfilment, joy, love, and peace, and also helps to create a positive backdrop for you to create your own reality.

Helping others to overcome their miasm debris is a blessing in disguise for them. It also spreads good vibration around their locality; restoring equilibrium to one and all, plus making everyone aware of how to live in good energy with all of its benefits.

REQUEST FOR TRANSMUTING MIASM DEBRIS

"Creator,

Benevolently bless all of my being with white Light, transmuting every aspect of negative presence, Grace replacing all, restoring harmony, peace and health. Bless my being with strength and fortitude, giving me complete creation.

Thank You."

Repeat this request aloud 3 times

REQUEST FOR TRANSMUTING
MIASM DEBRIS WITHIN BUILDINGS

"Creator,

I ask that you benevolently bless this building, transmuting all negative energy with white Light. Grace restoring all.

Thank You."

Repeat this request aloud 3 times

REQUEST FOR TRANSMUTING MIASM DEBIS FOR ANOTHER

"Creator,

I ask for transmutation for ……… Bless this soul with white Light. Relieve them of all negative presence, Grace replacing all.

Thank You."

Repeat this request aloud 3 times

MIASMS AQUIRED THROUGH KARMA

Miasms are extensive in various forms of negative energy. They have one thing in common: that is their ability to drain vitality, hope, and dreams, leaving their subject without the fire to move on in life. Karma can easily be accrued under these circumstances, adding weight to one's burdens. Without realising the enormity of the significant Laws governing our Universe, malevolent actions against another create karma.

These particular miasms can be found in a person's auric field throughout each layer, consequently affecting the corresponding part of the body, bringing past-life debt through to this incarnation. It is everyone's right within this particular lifetime to ask for release of previous karmic debt.

These particular miasms can remain with a soul for a number of lifetimes, but another, more tenacious, form is passed from generation to generation, giving no quarter. As one generation passes, younger members receive, giving the miasm fresh life.

Karmic miasms can make a person's existence that much more difficult. Taking control of one's journey is crucial for growth to occur.

REQUEST FOR RELEASE FROM
KARMIC DEBT

"Archangel Uriel,

I thank you for transmuting Karmic Miasms that are present within my auric field. Please let the Green Flame remove all   that is Karmic Miasm.

Thank You."

Repeat this request aloud 3 times

REQUEST FOR RELEASE FROM INHERITED MIASMS

"Archangel Metatron,

I thank you for transmuting the Inherited Miasms, which are in my auric field. Please let the Gold Flame remove all that is Inherited Miasm.

Thank You."

Repeat this request aloud 3 times

UNWANTED ENERGY

We are on a path throughout our lifetime to follow a chosen route. Each chosen route gives us the chance to improve how we think, how we behave, and how we teach our peers and children. On this journey, we meet many like-minded souls, as well as many who are not. It is this latter group of people that cause us testing times, so that we can, in effect, see just how much we have learned along the way. Each encounter brings to the fore problem areas that we need to address. If we find we are repeating certain scenarios, then we are not dealing with this particular issue, and must repeat it until the lesson has been taken on board. This causes us to buckle and lash out against the opposing individual. A miasmic energy then forms from the negative vibration of those involved. The vibration is instinctively felt by the receiving opponent, and responded to. Inevitably, a circuit of detrimental energy is created; continuing until one chooses to walk away. Sadly, once established, and regardless of time period, this circuit remains intact, leaving those involved permanently caught in its web.

Dissolving this destructive energy allows both participants to move on. If left, damage can affect all involved. Negative energy causes physical illness to occur; therefore, it is in everyone's best interest to release all to the Angelic realm.

REQUEST FOR DISSOLVING RECEIVED NEGATIVE ENERGY

"Archangel Zadkiel,

I ask that you benevolently dissolve all negative energy sent to me by ……… with Grace.

Thank You."

Repeat this request aloud 3 times

REQUEST FOR DISSOLVING
PERSONALLY SENT NEGATIVE ENERGY

"Archangel Zadkiel,

I ask that you benevolently dissolve all negative energy that I have sent to .... with Grace.

Thank You."

Repeat this request aloud 3 times

CHAPTER 6

AKASHIC RECORD

To describe an Akashic Record, it would be likened to a blueprint of a person's life. In fact, it is the blueprint for all of their existence throughout each lifetime experienced. Every soul on this planet has Angelic aid in the form of guiding, guarding and lastly, recording angels. The latter group maintains your personal file or Akashic Record, as it is known.

Akashic records preserve all information, allowing progress for each individual; every pre-birth plan is created with reference to this detailed source, ensuring aspects needed to create growth. Choices come into play throughout one's life giving responsibility to the individual. Therefore, each living person has total control over his or her own destiny, making crucial option part of the plan. Some have access to these records through practise, or are gifted in ability to do so; you too can gain accessible admission to view your own record.

If you decide you would like to do so, the first step would be to sit in a quiet room with no outside influence that may disturb you. Finding your breathing and slowing each breath, both inhale and expel to a comfortable level. Once you have achieved relaxation through careful, long and slow breathing, you can let your imagination take you to a secure, beautiful landscape of your choice. Once within your perfect place of peace, you may find a seated area to contemplate your worries. Here you can think through all aspects that cause you concern, knowing you have no outside opinions to influence your own thinking.

In this environment, it is possible to connect with your own recording angel. Take this opportunity to do just that. You may not see your angel, but feel its presence instead; know that you are secure and in the presence of love. Conversing with this Angelic being is simplified, as mind transference is often the selected medium for communication. Forming your question within your mind is enough to gain a response. Asking your question allows your angel to work on your behalf. After consulting your own record, you will be given the information through the most appropriate method of communication that you are able to recognise. Some will receive pictures in their mind's eye, others will hear a response, and lastly some may instinctively 'know' the answer. You can ask as many questions as you wish. Akashic records are not meant to be a secretive source, but others may not be allowed to view any other, unless they are high vibratory and given permission to do so pre-birth, primarily to enable others on their path. When you have finished with this time of communication, imagine you are zoomed back into your physical body. Wriggle your toes and fingers, stretch your limbs and begin to re-connect with your surroundings. Take time to drink water or coffee/tea, and eat if you feel a little woozy.

The request that you are about to read should be stated before you begin your relaxation, as it connects you directly to your recording angel who will ensure your complete safety whilst you meditate in this way.

REQUEST FOR CONNECTION BETWEEN YOUR AKASHIC RECORD AND YOUR RECORDING ANGEL

"Archangel Gabriel,

I ask to be connected to my Akashic Record through my Divine Recording Angel, allowing access will give me the information to benevolently help me on my Sacred Path. Please ensure my complete safety giving me Angelic protection.

Thank You."

Repeat this request aloud 3 times

CHAPTER 7

DISTANT HEALING

A loved one who lives miles away and falls ill can cause concern for other family members. Modern life has given everyone the ability to travel to distant shores on a daily basis. Many choose to move away, knowing they can return within a few hours. However, problems arise with the onset of illness. Family who would naturally help at such times may find it difficult; not many are able to drop everything to aid the ailing member.

If family members choose to request Angelic assistance, then the person in need of help can receive various healing rays. These rays enable recovery but in some instances, aid in the most appropriate course of action to fulfil the patient's highest need. Sometimes the highest need is not what you were looking for, as on occasion, passing to spirit occurs, which leaves everyone wondering 'why'. The time of any person's passing is never truly known, and regardless of age, always comes as a shock. Understand that before you were born, you choose your life and the people you are going to share it with. The Angelic realm cannot interfere with your 'blueprint' when it concerns key matters such as personal lessons. Requesting help for a person's highest need is always the main consideration when asking for support. This enables the most appropriate aid in assisting the ailing individual. This may be difficult to understand, as each individual has a pre-birth plan, necessary to enable that human being to experience all that is appropriate for his/her growth. This is the only limiting factor for the Angelic realm. All other occasions, regardless of their severity, can be alleviated with healing from the Divine.

Miles play no part in requesting aid; relief is given instantly, determining recovery. On occasion it is best to rally around other members of one's family, asking for all to request help. The more who do so, the more the healing process is strengthened. This applies to all who are sick or injured, whether distant or near at hand. Long-term aliments also fall into this category, alleviating the worst. All ailments or injuries are worth asking for Angelic assistance, as it comes in many guises.

REQUEST FOR DISTANT HEALING

"Archangel Raphael,

I ask that you benevolently bless ……… with Grace. Give him/her healing appropriate for his/her highest need; Divine blessing relieving all restoring health to his/her physical body.

Thank You."

Repeat this request aloud 3 times

REQUEST FOR HEALING ACCIDENTAL INJURY

"Archangel Raphael,

Please give .... benevolent healing allowing his/her highest need. Relieve all injuries with Grace, restoring all; Divine blessing allowing physical healing so he/she may recover fully.

Thank You."

Repeat this request aloud 3 times

CHAPTER 8

SICK EARTH ENERGIES

SICK BUILDING SYNDROME

Living in a home with areas of energy that may be making its occupants tired, irritable and, in extreme cases, physically ill, can affect the entire household; distressing all present, and creating uncomfortable surroundings. These are unacceptable conditions to be living within, and should be treated the same as woodworm, rising damp, or any other potential health risk. Making sure that your home is the safe, relaxed, pleasant place it is meant to be is essential to leaving you, your loved ones, and your pets feeling happy, recharged, secure, and ready to face the world once more.

Areas of any building that you feel uncomfortable to be in, but have only instinctive unease, may indicate 'sick building syndrome', as it is known as. Constant tiredness, headaches, feelings of irritation (for no apparent reason) and that have been medically assessed, may find their root cause lying with natural earth energy lines or other earth phenomena that is negatively aspected. Animals are always a good indicator to help spot any unnatural areas; dogs always avoid all forms of energy sources that are not in their best interest, whereas cats will curl up and happily sleep on them.

The Earth is gridded with energy lines. Some you may be familiar with, such as the Ley lines that our ancestors identified. Others such as Hartman lines, Curry lines and Energy lines have been labelled and identified by modern scientists, who have also realised that in some instances; these energy sources become negatively aspected, changing from a positive energy flow. The cause of such negative change varies from natural earth movement to man-made disruption, such as the planting of foundations for a new building/road/drain/ swimming pool, or any other form of excavating the earth. These lines become Black lines or Black Spots causing devastation when left. Other forms of natural earth energy include Energy Drains, Spirals, Fog and most importantly, underground water.

Our forefathers developed means of indicating both unhealthy and healthy sources of energy with simple methods of dowsing, using hazel twigs or similar wooden rods. Today, pendulums are commonplace. Although requiring patient practise, they reward the student with a link to esoteric knowledge, enabling a person to keep their home and workplace positive, free from any form of unhelpful energy. Returning to ancient methods of divining will aid our modern lifestyles, giving us a clear indication of how our planet affects us.

REQUEST FOR RESTORING POSITIVE ENERGY TO HOUSE OR BUILDING

(Includes Sheds, Outbuildings & Garages)

"Benevolently bless this house/building Father God, relieving all negative aspects permanently from the ground it stands upon, transmuting the energy to positive energy, permanently, filling the home with your permanent Grace and blessings radiating through. Allow all who live within your Divinity.

Thank You."

Repeat this request aloud 3 times

ELECTRICAL EFFECT ON BUILDINGS

In this age of modern technology, advances are permanently increasing on a day-to-day basis. On the whole, these advances make daily living persistently pleasurable; allowing constant interface with one's friends, family and the rest of the world alike. As well as gaining more time to work, play and holiday, site can have a wonderfully tranquil effect in maintaining equilibrium and good health, as the human physical body requires. The flip side of the coin in all of this is a constant barrage of electrical flow; one form or other hits the human field daily. The effect of this is a world weary before it rises; a western habit of modern day living, whereby homes are wired to generate the necessary electrical field to maintain constant source.

Allowing ourselves to perpetuate the twenty-first century way of life has a detrimental effect to the human field. When experienced, this impact lowers a person's resistance, leaving them open to disease and leading the way towards a life of related illness. Some modern forms of energetic flow are more cunning than those experienced so far. Both microwave cookers and WiFi connection leave the body weaker, creating a recipe for future ill health, and quickly achieving negative stasis. Returning to life without electricity is not an option at this moment in time, but living within a positive flow is.

REQUEST TO CHANGE TECHNOPATHIC STRESS INSIDE HOMES/BUILDINGS

"Creator,

Benevolently bless this house/building with beneficial resistant energy that transforms this house/building to a place of tranquillity making the change permanent. Allow all who live/work within positive health.

Thank You."

Repeat request aloud 3 times

OUTSIDE EARTH ENERGIES

Energy lines run around the globe, marking this planet with a natural grid. This energy is, for the most part, positively aspected and feeds the earth, making her a living being. This knowledge our ancestors were aware of, and utilised for their own needs.

Earthquakes and landslips above and below water sometimes change the natural flow of energy from a good aspect to unfavourable. When this occurs, the area becomes depleted of healthy stream, leaving, in some instances, a stagnant pool, which affects the area surrounding it. This also applies to land affected both by earthquakes and landslips.

Technopathic stress, (which is the name given to areas affected by electrical influence), also plays a huge part in dominating outside earth energies. Pylons and telephone masts that domineer our landscape can command changes to natural energy. Living with nullifying energy can have a very detrimental effect for both the Earth and humans alike.

One tell-tale sign of any form of negative energy includes trees bending out of the way of flow. Elder and ivy thrive under its influence, growing happily along its path. Ants take great delight from its presence as well. Livestock prefer a happier environment, clustering around beneficial energy, and also prefer healthy water;

thriving on its energetic influence. Instinct again plays a part as well as dowsing; the age-old method of verifying one's thoughts. Areas that are prone to accidents indicate a change of flow. Lastly, pockets of similar illness amongst a community indicate energy that is not working to benefit that district.

REQUEST FOR POSITIVELY CHANGING OUTSIDE EARTH ENERGIES

(To include areas of water)

"Creator,

Benevolently change earth energies to positive, leaving Mother Earth in balance permanently. These changes remain in place always.

Thank You."

Repeat this request aloud 3 times

REQUEST FOR TRANSMUTING TECHNOPATHIC STRESS OUTSIDE

"Creator,

Please will you transform the influence of resistant energy from negative to positive, changing permanently, benevolently blessing this area so Mother Earth is restored to health.

Thank You."

Repeat this request aloud 3 times

CHAPTER 9

PROTECTION

Each person alive today has an inner light, projecting what is reflected from within each being, and making visible shy, triple-interior plenary vitality. This divine light radiates continually, and protection may be required for those who test momently. In other words, the light that shines from everyone's interior can attract detrimental influence. Protecting oneself becomes part of a daily ritual, leaving no chance for mishap.

Daily protective request takes only moments of one's time, leaving all who do so secure in knowledge of Angelic presence. This information is necessary during this time, due to the sea of adverse energy that has tried to dominate our society. Calling for Angelic protection is the quickest method to aid someone, providing instant access to securing their being or that of another. Other forms of protection work in the same way; understanding why it is necessary is the key. Once taken on board, the method chosen can be completely personal.

At this moment in time personal transformation is the aim of many. This process, however, can make some feel very vulnerable. Protection is then essential, enabling the person with a suitable shield so that safety is maintained during the progression, allowing for smooth transition. The unfolding growth that this process gives can be enhanced with the Divine Grace that naturally occurs when a request for daily protection is made, giving dual benefits. Requesting a barrier against detrimental influence ensures complete enfoldment of the entire being from physical body, through all of the subtle body fields preventing all negative intrusion. This also applies to negative thought emitted by another, which in turn prevents a cycle of nullifying energy between people. Another benefit includes prevention of influence from another, freeing a person to follow his or her own path. Emotional persuasion can be damaging for the recipient. Without realising, they follow the will of another. If continued, their own choice may be completely overrun. It is vitally important within one's lifetime to be able to decide for oneself, as these choices help a person to grow.

Asking for Angelic protection can prevent disruption to certain places, such as buildings, hospitals and schools. Such places may also include local communities that have become no-go areas, rife with teenagers and children running wild and causing mayhem. Angelic help is essential here to restore peace, and to guide the participants to more worthwhile pursuits. If a couple of like-minded souls meet and request jointly protection for their neighbourhood, they turn the tide of adversity and create a new wave of energy to combat the dark shadow that has fallen over their community. Buildings can be protected as well, whether in the form of schools, hospitals, offices or any other communal building. Requests can be made to ensure a good place to learn, heal, work or socialise, whilst keeping vibrant energy throughout. Angelic forces do not discriminate towards any group. They are there to assist mankind, the animal kingdom, and the Earth; all we need do is ask.

When you call upon the Angelic realm, a form of angels surrounds you. These relay your message, immediately informing those needed. The appropriate angel then sets to work. If you already know who you wish to appeal to, they immediately respond. Archangel Michael is known as the 'Angel of Protection' and is depicted carrying a sword and shield. He is famous throughout history and amongst different religions for giving support to those who call out for help. He works with the Blue Ray, which includes a supportive anchor, capable of securing protection against physical and psychic attack; allowing all who ask 'Wreath of Complete Assistance'. Many have witnessed his work. The simple act of calling this Archangel ensures your safety in times of fear, and brings peace of mind to all who request help for loved ones.

Protection, therefore, is a multi-benevolent function; one that brings defence, freedom, growth, support and divine blessing. Just simply ask!

PROTECTION REQUEST FOR PERSONAL RELATIVES

"Archangel Michael,

I ask that a cloak of protection quickly surrounds my loved ones, repelling detrimental energy, keeping them safe in benevolent truth, all through this day/night.

Thank You."

Repeat this request aloud 3 times

PROTECTION REQUEST FOR PERSONAL USE

"Archangel Michael,

I ask that a protective bubble instantly surrounds me this day/night keeping me safe in God's Love and Light.

Thank You."

Repeat this request aloud 3 times

PROTECTIVE REQUEST FOR NEIGHBOURHOOD

"Archangel Michael,

I ask that a protective bubble be placed over this entire neighbourhood, now, keeping all in complete harmony through this day/night, holding benevolent force.

Thank You."

Repeat this request aloud 3 times.

PROTECTIVE REQUEST FOR HOME/WORKPLACE

"Archangel Michael,

I ask for a protective cloak to be placed over this house and garden/workplace this instant, keeping all within safe well away of all negative influence this day/night.

Thank You."

Repeat this request aloud 3 times

PROTECTIVE REQUEST FOR SCHOOLS/HOSPITALS/ COMMUNITY HALLS

"Archangel Michael,

I ask that a protective cloak be placed around this School/Hospital/ Community Hall, immediately, ensuring all within safekeeping from detrimental influence, enabling staff so they may work diligently.

Thank You."

Repeat this request aloud 3 times

CHAPTER 10

PLANETARY HEALING

Our world currently needs help so that ascension may be achieved. Earth is a living being in a cosmos of similar planetary bodies, all vital in course to each other. Understand how vital balance is to the Universe for ensuring stability. Hence the concern of our Angelic realms and universal neighbourhood, all wishing to aid Earth at this moment in time. Some cosmic neighbours experienced similar changes within their history. Having evolved, they wish their wisdom could be heard by those who may be influential, so that this transition proceeds smoothly for the good of all.

Angelic realms assist the planet with each prayer given by individuals. Prayer for the planet is vital, with each one being gratefully received and acted upon instantly. Praying allows the Angelic beings access to the healing source of the Universe, making this a necessary and significant act, which allows transition to flow. The healing source of the Universe allows not only vitality to reach therapeutic wants, but also strength, robustness and ability to change. This applies to all those receiving the Universal healing beams. Angelic work consists of aiding every living soul on this planet, including the planet herself and all of her living occupants:

animals, plants, trees, insects, water mammals, fish and creatures of the deep. Prayer allows and directs help to be given exactly where it is needed, making this process extremely simple, and therefore, absolutely essential to mankind. Over the last three decades, religious belief has waned, for whatever reason. New generations are consequently unaware of how the power of prayer works. This simple fact has created a rift, which has permitted a different society to emerge. Earth strains with mankind's negative outlook. Our collective actions, words, noxious thoughts and projections together affect all around us. This includes not only our schools, place of abode, and place of work, but also local towns, cities, pervading communities, countries, continents, and which may, if to continue in this way, globally cover our entire planet. Making a simple change in the way we think about life, ourselves and the people we share life with changes everything around us. This, in turn, affects those exact people; rippling outwards all the time, making collective impressions, beneficial to one and all. This collective energy aspires to make our world a better place to live in.

Angelic support can be given for individuals to help them make changes to their lifestyles. Enabling anyone in this way begins the turning of the tide. Requesting help for any individual is only prevented by one thing: pre-birth blueprint of a person's lessons necessary for their own progression. This will prevent Angelic intervention, but the prayer will go towards making this particular lesson easier, so that it is not wasted.

All of this is important to understand why Angelic-facilitating improvement contributes to the whole picture of planetary healing. By beginning with one single individual, everyone benefits including the planet.

The planet will survive the changes that are withholding progression. Aeons of time denote spiritual evolvement, giving Earth her rite of passage. Individuals who think outwardly can assist with requesting Angelic rhythm; they ultimately create ascension. Earth has set about making change. The last six decades have seen weather patterns change gradually, ocean currents flowing with more momentum, and movement in the earth's plates causing upward movement of land mass. All indicate physical transformation, which will increase over the next two decades, rising to a peak within the next 10 years. Our help in reducing mankind's neglect of one another ultimately facilitates Earth in lifting oppressive vibrations from her, relieving intolerable stress.

HEALING REQUEST TO RELIEVE OUR PLANET

"Archangel Metatron,

Benevolently release all detrimental strength from planet Earth with divine Grace, removing all that prevents her from ascending. Give healing where it is needed and bless her so that she may grow in Word.

Thank You."

Repeat this request aloud once only

HEALING REQUEST TO RELIEVE THE SEAS, OCEANS, ALL WATERS AND LAND

"Creator,

I ask that Grace be given to purify all Seas, Oceans and Land, relieving every living creature, mankind and the Planet. Give Divine blessing for restoring benevolent health so that all may live in harmony and understanding of your righteous scent.

Thank You."

Repeat this request aloud once only

HEALING REQUEST TO RELIEVE STRESS FROM PLANET EARTH

"Archangel Zadkiel,

Please relieve detrimental influence which inhibits ascension, benevolent Grace replacing all. Allow the Violet Flame precedence to transmute energy, giving relief and divinity so that vitality pervades all.

Thank You."

Repeat this request aloud once only

Printed in Great Britain
by Amazon